PAVILION

THE AMAZING
DINOSAUR
DETECTIVES

Fact orld

CONTENTS

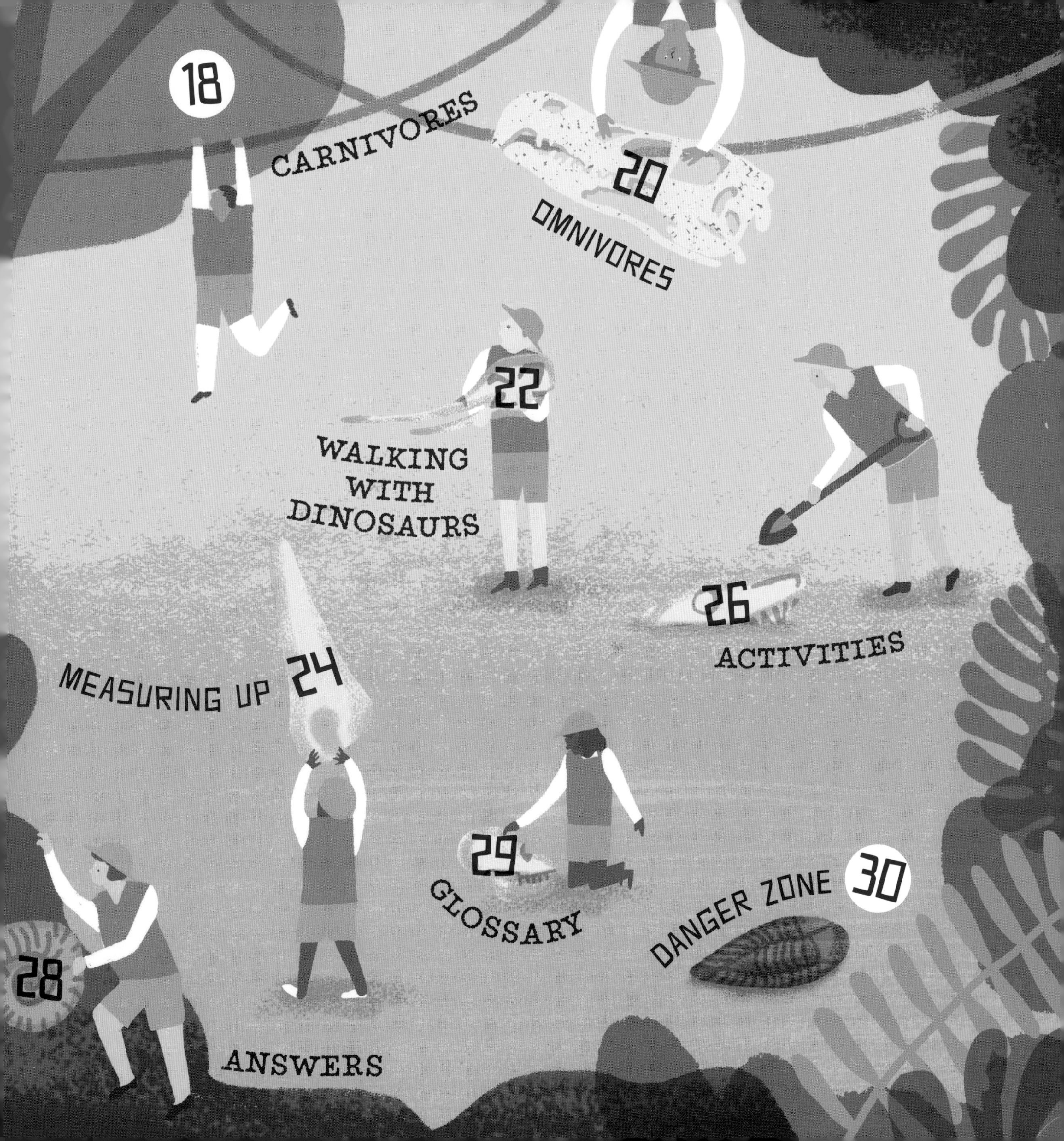

CALLING ALL DINOSAUR DETECTIVES

Are you ready to discover the world of dinosaurs and uncover lots of astonishing facts? Learn how to dig for bones, what parts of each dinosaur made them great, and the reasons why (most of them!) are not roaming our lands today.

Hi, I'm a **palaeontologist**

WHAT'S A... PALAEONTOLOGIST ?

A **palaeontologist** is a person who studies bones and **fossil** remains. They piece together clues about how **extinct** animals lived and behaved, and what they looked like. Each **fossil** or bone tells only part of the story, so it is a bit like putting together a jigsaw with lots of little pieces.

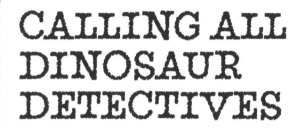

LAYERS OF EARTH

NOW!

yesterday

5 years ago

150 years ago

1 million years ago

145 million years ago

200 million years ago

250 million years ago

YOUR KIT BAG

These are some of the tools you will need to uncover the treasures lying beneath the ground.

TORCH

CHISEL

BRUSH

THE BONE WARS

Not only dinosaurs fought! So did the **palaeontologists** years ago in a battle that became known as THE BONE WARS!

THWACK
KA-POW
THWACK!

BUT WHAT WERE THE BONE WARS?

Two **palaeontologists** called E. D. Cope and O. C. Marsh had a competition to see who could find out the most about dinosaurs. They each wanted to win so badly that they cheated, stole and even destroyed dinosaur bones!

WHOOPS-A-DAISY

Even clever **palaeontologists** make mistakes. Each year we gather more and more information from new fossils and finds across the world. This means that we may believe one thing about dinosaurs only to have it proved wrong — we then have to update our records.

5. Millions of years later, the rock surrounding the skeleton is pushed to the surface (perhaps due to a volcano or earthquake) and is exposed, ready to be found!

1. Here's a squid swimming in the sea millions of years ago.

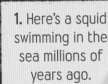

WHAT'S A... FOSSIL ?

A **fossil** is a bit of an animal or plant that has been in the ground for millions of years. Everything we know about dinosaurs comes from finding and understanding these **fossils**.

But I don't understand how a bit of an animal BECOMES a **fossil**?

4. As times goes by, new layers of earth and mud cover the remaining bones, burying them beneath the surface. This eventually turns to rock.

2. When the squid dies, its body sinks to the sea floor. Other sea animals eat the skin and flesh, leaving only the bones.

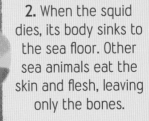

3. Some of these bones disintegrate leaving only the strongest bones.

A LAND BEFORE TIME

Dinosaurs lived millions of years ago. They also lived on the Earth for many years — so many, in fact, that this time has been divided into three ages called the Triassic, Jurassic and Cretaceous periods.

Dinosaurs were so successful that they ruled the Earth for around 160 million years. That's 800 times longer than we've been around.

ALL DINOSAURS LAID EGGS – FROM TINY EGGS ABOUT 3CM BIG TO SOME THE SIZE OF BASKETBALLS.

And to make it a bit more confusing...

BUT NOT MANY OF THESE EGGS HATCHED BECAUSE THEY WERE TASTY TREATS FOR OTHER DINOSAURS!

TRIASSIC
This is when the first dinosaurs started to appear. The land was warm with dry deserts covering most of the world. Life was hard so only the really TOUGH dinosaurs survived during these times.

THE MESOZOIC ERA
The Triassic, Jurassic and Cretaceous peroids are together known as the **Mesozoic** era.

300 MILLION YEARS AGO

TRIASSIC
250 MILLION YEARS AGO

DID YOU KNOW

?

'Dinosaur' is Greek for
* terrible creature
* terrible spider
* terrible lizard

CRETACEOUS
With volcanic activity increasing, flowering plants started to grow. This meant that there was an even larger variety of food to eat. Lots of dinosaurs lived and thrived during this period.

SEARCH FOR THE DINOSAUR WITH THE ANSWER!

JURASSIC
The world's **climate** was getting even warmer and wetter so plants started to grow very well. This made it easier for herbivores to survive. However, as they got plenty of food, the carnivores had more food too...

FACT OR FICTION

?

Most dinosaurs ate meat.

— FICTION!

DINOSAURS COULD LIVE TO BE OVER 100 YEARS OLD!

BUT WHAT HAPPENED NEXT?

Most dinosaurs were vegetarians (or herbivores).

ANSWER: TERRIBLE LIZARD

JURASSIC
200 MILLION YEARS AGO

CRETACEOUS
145 MILLION YEARS AGO

?

IT'S A MYSTERY

Around 65 million years ago the dinosaurs suddenly disappeared. There are many thoughts about why this happened.

Some people believe that a mystery bug made the dinosaurs feel ill and not many of them could fight it off. Those that didn't get better died.

MYSTERY BUG

BOOM
BANG
CRASH

ASTEROID IMPACT

Some people believe that a huge **asteroid** crashed into the Earth's surface, causing worldwide forest fires, tsunamis and enough dust to block out the sun for years. Nothing could grow so dinosaurs couldn't survive in these conditions.

BRRRRR

FREEZING COLD

Some people think that the **climate's** temperature changed and it got really cold, making it impossible for the dinosaurs to keep on living. They couldn't keep warm enough!

HOWEVER
SOME MAMMAL
INSECTS AND REPTILE
SURVIVED AND STILL LIV
WITH US TODAY... TURN T
PAGE 22 TO FIND OU

10

TYPES OF DINOSAUR

There were many types of dinosaurs ranging from two-legged quick runners to four-legged stompers.

Some dinosaurs ate meat, some ate plants, some ate both meat and plants. These three types of dinosaur have special names:

HERBIVORE = plant eater
CARNIVORE = meat eater
OMNIVORE = meat and plant eater

Keep reading to find out more!

CLASSIFICATION

SAUROPODS
Large herbivores that walked mainly on four legs

CERATOPSIANS
Medium-sized horned herbivores that walked on four legs

LARGE THEROPODS
Large carnivores that walked on two legs

ORNITHOMIMOSAURS
Ostrich-shaped herbivores or omnivores

SMALL THEROPODS
Small carnivores that walked on two legs

THYREOPHORA
Medium-sized herbivores that walked on four legs with armour and tail spikes

ORNITHOPODS
Medium-sized herbivores that usually walked on two legs

A WHAT-I-VORE?

I only want MEAT!

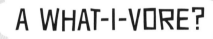

HERBIVORES

OMNIVORES

CARNIVORES

HEAVY ARMOURY

Dinosaurs had to be tough to survive. They developed ways to defend themselves and to attack their rivals and prey.

Some of these characteristics have been passed on to animals still living today. Have a look at crocodiles with their body **armour**, turtles with shells to protect themselves and hide away in, crabs with pincer claws, scorpions with a sting in the tail, horned animals like rhinos, and the tusks on elephants.

There were many different ways that a dinosaur could protect itself from being **prey**, including scaly skin, large spikes, and a very thick skull!

Great plates on its back were about the size of a dinner plate.

Not the cleverest dinosaur on the block!

The Stegosaurus had a very small brain. In fact, it was thought to be the same size as a ping pong ball.

The bony plates along its back may have been used to absorb heat from the sun, helping to keep it warm.

These dinosaurs didn't have teeth at the front of their mouths. Instead, they had a beak and then teeth further back for chewing things.

STEGOSAURUS STRENGHS!

SPIKES

HELMET

SHIELD ARMOUR

LONG SPIKY TAIL

The Ankylosaurus was huge and built like a tank — low lying and strong!

JUST IMAGINE
If you want to imagine what the Ankylosaurus's club-like tail did, think of a wrecking ball, knocking down a block of flats.

MEAN FIGHTING MACHINES
Battles between dinosaurs were often a matter of life and death. They developed features not only to protect themselves, but also to inflict maximum damage.

Spikes made it hard to be eaten!

Bony plates covered the eyes to protect them.

PARP!

The Ankylosaurus produced huge amounts of gas because of its diet.

The only way to defeat the Ankylosaurus was to flip it over — but that wasn't an easy thing to do!

ANKYLOSAURUS STRENGTHS!

SPIKES HELMET SHIELD ARMOUR CLUB TAIL

FLYING HIGH

Is it a bird? Is it a plane? No! It's a pterosaur! Technically, pterosaurs are not dinosaurs but they are related to them. In Greek, 'pterosaur' means 'winged lizard'. Unlike birds, they walked on their four limbs, like bats today.

Were pterosaurs like birds?

No! Birds have feathers. Pterosaurs had wings made out of skin, muscle and other tissues. Not a feather in sight!

Similar to lizards, pterosaurs had limbs that stick out from the sides of their bodies rather than underneath.

IT'S A MYSTERY!
One of the most distinctive features of Pteranodons, a type of pterosaur, was its backward-facing skull. But nobody has ever worked out why it was like this! Some people believe it was to help steering in flight, others believe it was to attract mates.

HOME SWEET HOME
Most pterosaurs lived in caves or trees.

THAT'S A MOUTHFUL
It is believed that some pterosaurs had up to 90 teeth in their mouths.

That's a lot of flossing!

BEST HEADDRESS COMPETITION

WELCOME

2   1   3

HOLLOW BONES?

Bones can be quite heavy, so pterosaurs developed hollow bones — bones that had very little in the middle — to make themselves lighter and therefore making it easier for them to fly!

DID YOU KNOW ?

The largest pterosaur was a Quetzalcoatlus. It had a wing span of 10 metres.

DID YOU KNOW ?

The first Pteranodon skull was discovered in 1876 in Kansas, U.S.A.

Pterosaurs are one of the most filmed creatures of this time (not forgetting the T-Rex)!

LIGHTS! CAMERA! ACTION!

WHAT DID THEY EAT?

In the first few months of life, pterosaurs ate insects. After this they would eat a lot of fish. They would fly low over the water and snatch up fish with their long beaks.

HERBIVORES

Dinosaurs that only ate plants, not meat, are called herbivores. They came in all shapes and sizes, and had unique characteristics to help them thrive in their world.

GUIDE TO SURVIVAL

Run, fly or swim away.

Hide (using camouflage).

Herbivores were tasty treats for the meat-eating dinosaurs. To not become **prey**, they had to...

FACT OR FICTION ?

Sauropods lived in herds.

|
FACT!

We lived in herds to try and protect ourselves from big carnivores, like the T-Rex.

WHAT'S A... SAUROPOD ?

Sauropods were the biggest land animals to ever have lived! They had small heads, long and flexible necks and massive bodies with long tails.

PHHOOO-EEE
Eating all that grass and plant matter meant that herbivores had a lot of wind to get rid of.

PARP!

PARPPP!

P A R P !

DID YOU KNOW ?

The Brachiosaurus could not chew. It had to swallow plants whole and then let its stomach break the food down into digestible chunks.

CARNIVORES

Dinosaurs that only ate meat are called carnivores. They were fierce and frightening creatures!

T-Rex had a very keen sense of smell and good eyesight — making it hard for **prey** to hide and get away!

LARGEST CARNIVOROUS DINOSAUR AWARD
Budge over T-Rex!
The winner is SPINOSAURUS!

2
1
3

MEAN MACHINE
The T-Rex could grow up to six metres tall and to about 12 metres long!

The T-Rex's arms were small compared with the rest of its body, but they were strong.

SCARIEST
DINOSAUR AWARD

Nobody knows if the tail was too heavy for the T-Rex to lift. It may have been dragged along the floor leaving a trail to be scared of!

The T-Rex was able to move quickly because of its massive legs and huge toes. It could reach speeds of around 25 mph.

KING OF THE DINOSAURS?
The name Tyrannosaurus Rex means 'tyrant lizard king' — and it was called this because it was one of the largest, meanest and most terrifying carnivores of all time!

Velociraptors had huge claws for hunting with.

FACT OR FICTION ?
The Spinosaurus was the first dinosaur to learn how to swim.

Look under the rock for the answer!

FACT!

WHO ARE YOU CALLING CHICKEN? Velociraptors had feathers, not scaly skin like most dinosaurs. They were the same size as a large chicken. But mean...

Velociraptor means 'SPEEDY THIEF'.

OMNIVORES

Dinosaurs that ate both meat and plants are called omnivores. They shared features with both carnivores and herbivores.

BEST OF BOTH WORLDS

Omnivores had a high chance of survival because they could eat whatever was available. Whether meat or plants were on offer, they could tuck in!

GO!

COLD TURKEY

Heterodontosaurus fossils are hard to come by, but it is thought they were about same size as a turkey.

DID YOU KNOW ?

The Oviraptor, when fully grown, was about the same height as a child — just like you (around 120 to 150cm)!

Goes to the TROODON!

Troodons had large brains for their body size, making them one of the cleverest dinosaurs.

BEAK FACE

A few dinosaur fossils have been found with bird-like beaks. These helped omnivores to eat both plants (picking seeds out of pods) and meat (ripping it from the bone).

BRAINEST DINOSAUR AWARD

CLAW TASTIC
The Therizinosaurus had three gigantic claws at the end of forelimb, which could have been used to strip bark from trees.

GO TROODONS

39

23

FASTEST DINOSAUR AWARD
Goes to all the ORNITHOMIMOSAURS!
(Some could run up to 43 mphl)

ALL MIXED UP
Heterodontosaurus means 'lizard with different teeth'. Most dinosaurs have just one kind of tooth but this one had three: small teeth for chopping off leaves, teeth for chewing, and two pairs of long, canine-like teeth.

EGG THIEF?
Oviraptor means 'egg thief' because it was once thought that they stole eggs to eat. However, it is now thought that they nested on their eggs and cared for them but the name remains

WALKING WITH DINOSAURS

When dinosaurs roamed the Earth, so did a lot of other creatures. Some of these creatures are still around today.

FACT OR FICTION ?

A long time ago, some crocodiles lived on a vegetarian diet.

FACT!

BEES

Bees may have survived the big event that wiped the dinosaurs out because they make their homes underground or in sheltered areas.

The Simosuchus ate leaves and was no bigger than a small dog!

CROCODILES AND ALLIGATORS

Mr Snappy hasn't changed his looks much since the time of the dinosaurs.

Other creatures that lived with the dinosaurs include crabs, snails, lobsters, sharks and frogs!

Duck-billed platypus lay eggs, even though they are mammals.

FACT!

SEA STARS

A star that's alive without a brain? This creature is quite amazing. It isn't often eaten by **predators** because it's covered in bony skin (so it's not very tasty!). It can also grow back an arm if it loses one!

No wonder they have survived so long!

DUCK-BILLED PLATYPUS

This is one of the most unusual animals alive. It has a beak like a duck, a body like an otter and tail similar to a beaver.

WARNING! The male has a venomous spur on each of its hind feet for defending itself.

How very odd!

CHEEKY CUSTOMER When they find food, they store it in their cheeks until they can eat it in safety away from other predators.

They are from a special group of mammals called MONOTREMES. That's a big word for a mammal that lays eggs rather than giving birth to live young.

DON'T BE FOOLED! Even though they look sweet, they are still carnivores.

23

MEASURING UP

It's easy to think that all dinosaurs were huge, terrifying creatures. As it happens, that's not the case and some were smaller than we are!

TALL AND MIGHTY
The Brachiosaurus really was a huge dinosaur!

DID YOU KNOW ?
Not only was the Brachiosaurus very tall, it was as long as two buses!

SPINOSAURUS

STEGOSAURUS

Don't be fooled by the Velociraptor's height — it was deadly!

GOOD SPREAD
Pterosaurs came in all shapes and sizes.

REWIND
◄◄
Each of the dinosaurs shown here feature on an earlier page. Can you go back and find them?

PERSPECTIVE
Use our bus to help work out just how tall these dinosaurs were.

SOMETHING SPECIAL?
Whatever their shape and size, all dinosaurs had amazing features that made them great! Can you remember what was special about these three?

T-REX

ACTIVITIES

Now that you have learned about lots of different dinosaurs, it's time to have a think and see if you can solve these mysteries!

GUESS THE DINOSAUR

1.
I'VE GOT SUPER SHARP TEETH AND I'M SOMETIMES CALLED THE KING OF THE DINOSAURS.

2.
MY NECK IS SO LONG I CAN REACH THE TOP OF THE TREES.

3.
I'M ONE OF THE FASTEST DINOSAURS AROUND.

4.
MY BRAIN IS THE SIZE OF A PING PONG BALL.

5.
I AM THE SAME SIZE AS A CHILD.

6.
I AM THE FIRST DINOSAUR TO LEARN HOW TO SWIM.

MAKE YOUR OWN FOSSILS

Why not try making your own fossils at home? Find a large plastic bin, fill it with bits of mud, rocks and grass. When it is half full, add in some washed chicken bones, or spare ribs, or toys that you want your friends to find. Cover them up with more mud, rocks, grass and earth. When you're done, enjoy digging up your hidden treasures with friends!

THE ANSWERS ARE
OVER THE PAGE IF
YOU GET STUCK!

SPOT THE DIFFERENCE

Can you spot the six differences between these two pictures?

DINO WORD SEARCH!

Can you find the hidden words inside the grid?

CARNIVORE

OMNIVORE

T-REX

DETECTIVE

PTERANODON

HERBIVORE

SAUROPOD

E	H	Y	E	C	R	D	O	X	H
P	T	E	R	A	N	O	D	O	N
L	B	F	O	R	O	P	F	N	O
R	C	H	V	N	M	O	G	V	E
O	A	B	I	I	N	R	C	A	C
T	Q	Y	B	V	I	U	Y	M	X
S	E	L	R	O	V	A	U	E	P
F	F	W	E	R	O	S	R	P	X
H	P	S	H	E	R	T	V	A	C
E	V	I	T	C	E	T	E	D	P

GUESS THE DINOSAUR

3.
I'M ONE OF THE ORNITHOMIMOSAURS!

5.
I'M AN OVIRAPTOR.

2.
I'M A BRACHIOSAURUS.

4.
I'M A STEGOSAURUS.

6.
I'M A SPINOSAURUS.

1.
I'M A T-REX.

SPOT THE DIFFERENCE

DINO WORD SEARCH!

E	H	Y	E	C	R	D	O	X	H
P	T	E	R	A	N	O	D	O	N
L	B	F	O	R	O	P	F	N	O
R	C	H	V	N	M	O	G	V	E
O	A	B	I	I	N	R	C	A	C
T	Q	Y	B	V	I	U	Y	M	X
S	E	L	R	O	V	A	U	E	P
F	F	W	E	R	O	S	R	P	X
H	P	S	H	E	R	T	V	A	C
E	V	I	T	C	E	T	E	D	P

ARMOUR

The parts of a dinosaur's body that were used to defend itself from other dinosaurs — like spikes, plated skin, and thick skulls.

PREDATOR

A fearsome animal that hunts or kills other animal for food.

PREY

An animal that is hunted and killed by another animal for food.

ASTEROID

A rock from outer space. An asteroid can be small or very large.

FOSSIL

The preserved remains of plants and animals.

PALAEONTOLOGIST

A person who studies bones and fossils trying to work out who they belonged to, what they looked like, and how they lived. They try to create a picture of the world before we lived on it.

CLIMATE

The general temperature and weather conditions over a long peroid of time.

MESOZOIC ERA

This is the time from about 250-65 million years ago when the dinosaurs ruled the Earth. It is divided further into the Triassic, Jurassic and Cretaceous periods.

EXTINCT

When every last creature in a species dies out.

GLOSSARY

DANGER ZONE

Do you dare to play among the dinosaurs? Watch out for a swamp, an egg thief and a T-Rex!

START

ENTER THIS WAY

Egg thief! Miss a go.

New discovery! Take a short cut.

KEEP OUT!

Fall into the swamp! Move back.

Hop on a raptor. Move ahead 2 spaces.